THIRTY DAYS OF CONTEMPLATIVE MEDITATIONS

with the

Wesleyan Contemplative Order

Volume One

I0159880

Editor

Don Carroll

The author expresses his appreciation to his collaborators Ann Ehringhaus and Wayne Morris for their creative photographic expression in the interactive "CONNECT" journals (available at: www.practicesofawareness.com) which provided the inspiration for many of the meditation texts here, and particularly for WCO Magdalene Band members Anne Gilchrist for her help and encouragement in giving life to these particular meditations and to Lisa Marion and Mary Taylor for their keen editing help.

"You wander in a spiritual bazaar picking up a hundred items. Buy something!"

Rumi

MY REFLECTIONS:

Day 1

Beginning the Journey

"Neither do people pour new wine into old wineskins. If they do, the skins will burst; the wine will run out and the wineskins will be ruined. No, they pour new wine into new wineskins, and both are preserved."

Matthew 9:17

While there are spiritual solutions to life issues at any age, it is primarily in the second half of life that we come to grips with our spiritual journey. (Trauma or chronic illnesses, like alcoholism, can force us to do this at a much earlier age.) What appears to be a call to a spiritual journey too early in life can be an effort to escape from some aspect of emotional growth caused by serious early childhood wounding. In such cases the path of avoidance may be an intense and profound experience, but the spiritual journey will be a bit circuitous.

Once we begin a spiritual journey, it is always an experiential process. There is no figuring it out in the head by analyzing and thinking. The spiritual process is by definition a lived process since it involves us bodily, mentally, emotionally and spiritually—in fact it is as a spiritual process that all of these aspects of our humanness are tied together in a coherent way.

The first step in this process is often a rejection of old ideas, or a new way of understanding the ideas that we grew up with and sustained us earlier in life. This is appropriate and developmentally correct, for in the early years our task was to build a way to understand ourselves in the outer world. We needed to develop an ego.

For the less religiously oriented of us, the first step on the spiritual journey may be a realization that our egos—what we accomplish, what we say and do, are not sufficient to make us feel fulfilled—that there is still something missing. For those growing up in a religious tradition, it is coming to the intuitive understanding that our religious belief system, our religious dogma, if you will, does not explain our life in a sufficient way—that there is still something missing.

In both cases, the Self, whether it is of a non-believer or a believer, realizes that the experience of the ego self is incomplete. So the spiritual journey begins when we realize that no matter what we have accomplished, how many people like us, whatever fame, power or fortune we have acquired—something is still missing. It is with the mystery of something unknown missing that the spiritual journey begins.

<u>Practice</u>: Reflect on whether you have every-thing in your life or is something missing?

MY REFLECTIONS:

Day 2

The Being Mystery

"Since you have taken off your old self with its practices and have put on the new self, which is being renewed in knowledge in the image of its Creator."

Colossians 3:9-10

However we begin our spiritual journey—pulled along by the feeling of something missing or caught in a liminal space—over time we come to experience that there is a being Self, not a part of our ego, that is watching our life and is the key to our spiritual journey. The being Self has a sense of our life passing by, but it does not seem to grow old. It is the part of the Self that is connected to the Mystery of creation, outside of the ego, which is timeless.

I once heard "patience" described as one of the essential prerequisites of maturity. My immediate thought was that I will never make it. Now it is my perspective that patience is simply a by-product of identifying more deeply with the being Self that is always in the present moment. The unknowability of the being Self stems from the fact that we only experience it as a perspective on our life from our ground of being. We do not have another internal perspective from which to observe it. Thus, it is always a part of the Mystery of our life that connects us with Mystery outside of ourselves. The realization experience of the being Self is the first stage of our spiritual journey.

Practice: Reflect on your awareness of the ineffable Mystery of your being Self?

MY REFLECTIONS:

Day 3

The Connection of the being Self to Mystery

"And to put on the new self, created to be like God in true righteousness and holiness...for we are all members of one body."

Ephesians 4:24-25

The second stage in our spiritual journey is an experience that the being Self is connected to the being Mystery of all other humans. For some people that experience is a realization of connection with all sentient beings. Since the being Self is never experienced as object, it never experiences the Mystery of other being selves as objects; rather they are experienced as connected to the same Mystery as that in which the being Self itself participates. Once we put this being Self into the dogma of a scheme of belief, it will get different names—the transpersonal self, Christ Consciousness, Buddhahood and so on.

In Christian terms, Hell is identification with the limited ego self. Identification with the ego self is the result of sin, or a falling short of not being able to identify with the being Self, so one is caught in identification with the ego. Heaven, on the other hand, is identification with the Mystery of the being Self. For Christians that is experienced as living in connection with the Holy Spirit, or living in the Presence of God. Jesus of Nazareth was divine because he, more than anyone else, lived from the being Self that is the Mystery. We all have this same divine spark, non-ego being Self, even if it is buried deep under a self-determined ego.

The mystics in all different traditions have developed practices suited for their cultures that allowed them to move into the experience of the being Self. Their stories recount afterwards the blissful nature of such experiences. But they never are able to describe the experience while in such states, because once the state is made an object of consciousness the connection is lost.

<u>Practice</u>: Reflect on how you might more deeply experience connection to the Mystery of what is more than you?

MY REFLECTIONS:

Day 4

We Question to Grow

"Teacher," he asked, "what must I do to inherit eternal life?"

Luke 10:25

We move from an ego-centered life to a more being centered life, when we begin to ask the question: "What does life want me to do?" Or, "What does God want me to do with my life?" Or, "Why am I here?" Or, "If I thought I knew my life's purpose, is it today what I thought it was yesterday?"

Developmentally, we should not skip learning a skill, knowing how to make a living, learning to be responsible for our livelihood in this world. This process of practical learning is somehow a prerequisite to moving beyond the ego's full grasp. But once we have the ego survival skills in place, we all begin to ask larger questions. Sometimes these larger questions seem to be tied to issues of fame, power or money. In that case, the ego is still in charge, just the questions have been super-sized.

But asking the question fiercely, "What is my life for?" is always sure to move us to a deeper level in our spiritual journeys. Just asking the question begins to cut away some of the ego's stubborn scaffolding. Just asking the question begins to move us more deeply into the Mystery of our own lives.

<u>Practice:</u> Reflect on what your being asks of you today?

MY REFLECTIONS:

Day 5

The Capacity of the Heart

"Blessed are the pure in heart, for they will see God."

Matthew 5:8

The ancient wisdom is that the mental faculty of the mind is not the organ by which we further our spiritual journey. The mind is a wonderful thing, and like many of our human abilities does yeoman service for us in figuring out ways to cope with things in our lives. But it is not the organ by which we gauge our spiritual journey. Just as we don't try to employ the hands to do what the feet do, so we find that we suffer if we try to get the mind to replace the being as the organ that navigates our spiritual journeys.

Whenever we turn our spiritual journeys over to our minds, we always end up in a crisis of faith. This makes sense. The mind is the organ that, despite all its wonderful characteristics and problem solving abilities, worries. The mind/ego is the part of us that has resentments, that believes all things should work out for the better and has a picture of what that better ought to be.

In the real world we arrive, make connections, do things and die. The mind stumbles at the boundaries of this reality—the beginning and end don't ever really make rational sense. Our spiritual journey is about coming to terms with what does not make logical sense. It is important to understand that the organ to do this with is not the mind but the heart. We spend a lot of time in our lives training the mind. Most of us spend very little time on the task of increasing the capacity for the heart to understand. It is from our heart that the energy of our beingness flows. Nature always moves us in a direction of growth and when we finally come to consider where we are in our own spiritual journeys, we begin the process of growing the capacity of the heart.

Practice: Reflect on whether you manage your spiritual journey with your mind or your heart.

MY REFLECTIONS:

Day 6

The Beauty Touchstone

"One thing have I asked of the Lord, that will I seek after; that I may dwell in the house of the Lord all the days of my life, to behold the beauty of the Lord."

Psalm 27:4

Our spiritual journeys start and end with our relationship to Beauty, Truth and Goodness. These are the three Platonic virtues and these virtues arise from the three centers of intelligence which bring us to God—emotional intelligence, mental intelligence and somatic intelligence. Let's start at the beginning of this journey with Beauty. Our childhood spiritual beliefs arise around our experience of the order, harmony, and, if you will, the Beauty of the universe. The mental process of understanding our beliefs is not what gives us our beliefs. Our beliefs are a product of our experience. They involve our whole being as distinct from just our reasoning capacity. So while our beliefs do not produce our spiritual journeys, they do serve as markers along the way of our spiritual experience.

Early religions spent much time and effort and ritual predicting and trying to be in harmony with the seasons of the year. Man looked to the orderliness of nature through patterns of animal migration to provide food to sustain life and through patterns of rain and sunshine to grow corn, beans and other basic crops. Certain religious rituals emerged around giving thanks for the orderliness of nature that provided the necessary sustenance for life. Another set of religious rituals emerged around trying to implore the gods to restore a natural harmony when it seemed that droughts, floods or other natural events had upset the balance necessary for survival.

Our most basic and primitive spiritual instinct then has to do with our survival, for a yearning for orderliness in life. There is Beauty in the birth of each new dawn, in the return of the season of spring and the abundance of summer.

Our spiritual journeys begin when in some way we recognize and honor the importance of the harmony and Beauty of the natural world.

One of the reasons that threats of global warming and ecological disaster penetrate so deeply to our souls is that they threaten the most primal experience of our spirituality.

Practice: Reflect on how you recognize and honor the importance of harmony and Beauty in the natural world?

MY REFLECTIONS:

Day 7

Beauty as a Spiritual Path

"And you shall tend upward only, and not downward; if you obey the commandments of the Lord your God, which I command you this day..."

Deuteronomy 28:13

From the orderliness of nature, man developed a sense of inner orderliness, of conscience. We learned morals. We learned the standards of conduct that allowed for an orderly social process. We learned a sense of right and wrong, of rules to protect the weak in society and rules to prevent the abuse of power by the powerful. As a social organism we have incorporated the laws of nature into our social order. Rules of survival have, through much fine tuning, become codes of chivalry and books of etiquette. The Beauty of nature's orderliness has become a way to preserve an orderly society.

Our religious traditions evolved complex rules to help maintain this God given orderliness of nature in our social interactions. As instructive and helpful as these rules may be, their meaning for us lies in our ability to tap the experience of Beauty which is their source.

Practice: Reflect on how you appreciate Beauty as a connection with something greater than yourself.

MY REFLECTIONS:

Day 8

How Early Beliefs Can Become Stumbling Blocks

"We have been released from the law so that we serve in the new way of the Spirit, and not in the old way of the written code."

Romans 7:6

When the rain of mental discoveries began to shower us in the seventeenth and eighteenth centuries, this age of enlightenment gave birth to the idea of deism. This is the notion that, like the mechanical devices that were then being discovered and put to use, God was the great watchmaker in the sky that set the earth and planets in motion but was otherwise absent from the world. His presence was only the effect of the laws of mechanical theory. Deism is a religious theory designed by the mind to satisfy the mind's sense of orderliness and harmony. It is a wonderful theory, but it does nothing to satisfy the soul.

Deism is a sophisticated extension of the way primitive religions tried to provide a framework for the orderliness of nature. Most of us at some time are enchanted by the idea of God creating and setting in motion this world governed by exquisitely precise operating laws. But this belief does nothing to help us in time of human need.

Practice: Reflect on how your need for orderliness of belief affects your spiritual growth.

MY REFLECTIONS:

Day 9

The Experience of Divinity

"God is with you in everything you do."

Genesis 21:22

To move beyond the limitations of the mind in our spiritual journeys, we all first become pantheists. Pantheism regards the universe as a manifestation of God. It says there is a spark of God in everything. We don't become pantheist by trying to figure out our beliefs in our heads. We become pantheist because we (and here I mean the big we, all people) regularly experience moments of connection, wonder and Beauty with the world and others.

One of the more vivid of these experiences occurred in 1973 when astronaut Edgar Mitchell was part of the Apollo 14 mission. During the three-day journey back to Earth aboard Apollo 14, Mitchell had an epiphany while looking "down" on the earth from space: "The presence of divinity became almost palpable, and I knew that life in the universe was not just an accident based on random processes...the knowledge came to me directly." Mitchell's experience became famous because he was looking at the earth from space, but such experiences, though perhaps not with the grandeur of Mitchell's, have occurred for all of us in experiencing a sunset or the birth of a child. They are uncommon common experiences that connect us with the divinity that underlies all human experience. With recognition of these experiences, we jump individually, and historically, from a survival experience of God, to a being experience.

<u>Practice</u>: Reflect on how your conscious beliefs about God tell you about how you are experiencing your spiritual journey.

MY REFLECTIONS:

Day 10

Chaos and our Experience of God

"God will stretch out over Edom the measuring line of chaos and the plumb line of desolation."

Isaiah 34

In our movement from a survival experience of God, to a social experience, to a mental experience, to a being experience, we have stayed in the realm of understanding God as part of orderliness and harmony. This is only half the equation of life—the other half is disorganization and chaos. This second half is when we really get into the emotional stew of our spiritual journey. We experience a profoundly disorganizing event: a child dies before the parent, we lose a loved one in a totally random accident.

How we come to understand such life-changing, dis-organizing events profoundly affects our spiritual journeys. While not in any way discounting the importance of the grief process, when it takes time to live through such profoundly disorganizing events, at some point we have to come to terms with the spiritual meaning of this chaos. This is an inner journey. We have moved from the outer world of our spiritual journey with its focus on orderliness to an inner world.

The Mystery of the spiritual meaning of our inner world comes out of our encounter with our own inner chaos. This inner chaos is always there, but often it is a chaotic external event that triggers the beginning of this internal journey.

<u>Practice</u>: Reflect on how you resist the call of the Mystery of your own internal chaos. Reflect on how you respond to emotional chaos in your life in relation to your spiritual beliefs.

MY REFLECTIONS:

Day 11

Chaos as a Prelude to Renewal

"He saved us, not because of righteous things we had done, but because of his mercy. He saved us through the washing of rebirth and renewal by the Holy Spirit."

Titus 3:5

Chaos is not easy stuff. On one level we all hate it, and do our utmost to push it away. Yet there is in our soul a part of us that intuitively understands that it is through chaos that we pursue the second half of our spiritual journey.

Uncertainty has a way of leveraging our personal choices. If all were just orderliness, with no unexpected loss and unanticipated grief, then our egos could in actuality pretty much handle our lives. But unexpected loss and unanticipated grief are part of the nature of life. We are born and we bond with people we love and we lose them, sometimes in a seemingly natural progression and at other times for what will always seem the most arbitrary of reasons.

Through the chaos of life, we are initiated into a deeper level of spiritual reality. We can of course refuse this initiation. We can get stuck in "why me?" or some other ego-centered appraisal of the impact of the arbitrariness of life. Or, we can begin to gradually abandon our egos by devotion to spiritual practices that offer us meaning through the chaos.

Often our spiritual journeys begin with a serious illness, or some sort of life trauma, that forces us to seek, not rational meaning, but spiritual meaning in uncertainty. This does not mean that we have to wait to get bludgeoned by some chaotic event to get to the brass tacks of our spiritual lives. Quite the contrary, those who have undertaken spiritual practices such as prayer and meditation in the more orderly times of their lives, have a real step up when chaos and uncertainty strike. Chaos will come. It always does. Just like orderliness, it is a primary aspect of life. And just as Beauty emerges from our spiritual encounter with harmony, so also does Beauty emerge from our spiritual encounter with chaos.

<u>Practice</u>: Reflect on where the experience of chaos has taken you to a deeper level of understanding and connection with God?

MY REFLECTIONS:

22

Day 12

God's Love

"But perfect love drives out fear, because fear has to do with punishment. The one who fears is not made perfect in love."

1 John 4:18

At a time of uncertainty and chaos in our lives, we make choices. We can escape the invitation of chaos by avoidance in the many charming guises of work, indulgences in food, sex or drink, or fantasy. Or, we can allow the encounter with uncertainty to christen our dedication to a greater consciousness.

We wish to be free of the fears of uncertainty—free of the fear of not having a good enough job, of not having enough money, of not finding and/or keeping the right mate. To be free of fear, we have to learn to trust. In fact, a yearning to be able to trust life is an unconscious pull that often gets us started on our spiritual journeys. We want to be able to trust that life is and will be okay.

Both the possibility and the reality of uncertainty and chaos pose spiritual opportunities. We want to be free of the need to control, to be free of the fear of not being good enough, to be free of the need for approval. We in essence want freedom from all the things that the ego thinks it needs to be okay. We want to be enough, to belong, to be accepted by something greater than ourselves.

We want connection with what is greater than ourselves. We want our own wholeness and connection with what we intuit is a divine force that holds that wholeness.

As our spiritual journey deepens, we may realize that we want to connect with a loving and caring God.

Practice: Reflect on your willingness to answer the questions that your uncertainty asks of you?

MY REFLECTIONS:

Day 13

The Inner Journey

"But his bow remained steady, his strong arms stayed limber, because of the hand of the Mighty One of Jacob, because of the Shepherd, the Rock of Israel"

Genesis 49:24

Once we commit ourselves to the possibility of greater connection to consciousness and meaning in the world, we invite in all the possibilities that chaos offers. This is the focus of the contemplative practice of Welcoming Prayer.

Chaos theory is defined as the branch of mathematics that deals with complex systems whose behavior is highly sensitive to slight changes in conditions, so that small alterations can give rise to strikingly great consequences. In theological terms through the alignment of our conscious intentions with a meaning greater than ourselves, we open ourselves up to the possibility of Grace. Grace is the Beauty that comes from chaos.

At this stage of our spiritual journeys, our lives may seem outwardly as ordinary as ever, but the interior journey has begun in earnest. A sure sign is experiencing a calling, that we are called to do something special in this world (something special in the sense that somehow we are especially suited to do it). This something special may be quite ordinary, but will offer us a way to have a greater experience of the Beauty of our creative interaction with others and the Divine.

<u>Practice</u>: How am I open to the chaos in my life as a way to God?

MY REFLECTIONS:

Day 14

Training for the Journey

"It was Preparation Day, and the Sabbath was about to begin."

Luke 23:54

To be good at sports, an athlete has to train. To progress in one's spiritual journey, the discipline of training is also necessary. Like athletic training, spiritual training is developmental. The most helpful training depends upon where we are along the road. The formula of the twelve steps of Alcoholics Anonymous gives a good recipe for the first stages.

In the first stage, we come to believe at an emotional level that we don't have all the answers and that there is help outside of ourselves in finding greater wisdom for our lives. Next, we do a thorough job of becoming aware of all the patterns in our life that limit our connection to self, God and others. These patterns are largely based upon fears—fear of material insecurity, emotional insecurity and social/sexual insecurity.

Once we understand the patterns by which we try to protect ourselves from our fears and insecurities, we become willing to let go of these patterns. Then we review our life, and wherever we have caused harm, we go back (as long as it will not create more harm) and make amends—that is, we set things right. We engage in restorative justice. Only after all this has been done are we ready for the next level of spiritual training. This next level focuses on prayer and meditation.

The Twelve Steps of Alcoholics Anonymous make clear that listening silently for God will not be that productive if we have not first sought to remove our emotional defenses that block us from ourselves and God, clearing our psychic attics and basements of old resentments and guilts. It is hard to wait silently on God when our emotions keep coming back to feelings of guilt and shame.

In other words, before the radio transmitter of the soul can be tuned into God, we have to get rid of all the static and interference caused by the defenses we created to help us survive, and right the wrongs that we have done because of those emotional defenses. Once the interference is cleared up, then the possibility of communication with something greater than self begins in the silence of our hearts.

Practice: Reflect on whether you have done the initial stage work of clearing your mind and emotions so you can be available to dialogue with God?

MY REFLECTIONS:

28

Day 15

Trust

"Blessed is the one who trusts in the Lord, who does not look to the proud, to those who turn aside to false gods."

Psalm 40:4

Once the basic work of clearing old patterns has been done, what is the training regime like for the next phase of our spiritual growth?

The bad news is that a focus on mental prayer, listening to tapes of your favorite mentor or reading the next must-read spiritual book is not going to be sufficient. The good news is that by now, once we are in a cleared state, our longing for an experience of God is deeper, feels more fundamentally a part of who we are. It is a dual longing that may be experienced simply as a sense of yearning. The two aspects of this longing are the pull toward knowing God and the pull toward knowing the spark of divinity within ourselves.

We begin to sense that finding our own greatest potential is tied up with experiencing emotional freedom. To arrive at a place of emotional freedom, we must experience the world as safe, that all is truly okay. To feel free we must have an emotional reality that sees all the suffering in the world, and still believes deeply in the goodness of our lives. We no longer fear being ourselves and we no longer fear God. The aspects of our spiritual life that we must strengthen to be in the place of liberation, or nirvana or Heaven on Earth, are our faith and our courage.

We build faith by daily seeking to increase our trust. Trust is built by practices of thankfulness. We build courage by daily taking small risks that move us closer to ourselves, to God and to others.

Practice: Reflect on the risks you are willing to take today to move closer to self, God and others?

MY REFLECTIONS:

Day 16

Discernment

"After forty years had passed, an angel appeared to Moses in the flames of a burning bush in the desert near Mount Sinai."

Acts 7:30

On our spiritual journeys, we would all love to have a Moses burning bush experience. Many of us have prayed, particularly in a time of need or uncertainty: "God tell me what to do?" "What is my truth?" Foxhole prayer is not usually the way that we are led to connect with a wisdom greater than ourselves.

Some of us are born and grow up with an easy access to an intuitive sense of knowing. It is heart knowledge. Or gut knowledge. Over time, we learn that it is sometimes not right, and that we may need to get a second opinion, but we learn that we can rely on our deeper inner intuitive sense of knowing most of the time.

Others of us, some-times in childhood, were made to feel that this intuitive sense of knowing was not right, or could not be believed. As adults we don't have easy access to this place of connection to our own wisdom, or if we do, we don't trust it.

We may have a certain pervasive anxiety that keeps us from being able to fully access our own wisdom. Many of us with this kind of childhood wounding have a special gift for the nuances of truth, but must give some dedicated time to learning to trust our gut and being wisdom.

If intuitive knowing is weak, we just start practicing. In ordinary decisions, rather than making a mental habit decision, we take a moment to focus on our heart, or gut, to see what sense of a decision comes from that place. Following the arc of decisions made from a more intuitive place–what sort of outcomes are there? How do these outcomes compare with decisions just made out of mental habit?

Practice: Am I able to connect with my inner sense of knowing? Am I willing to work to strengthen the muscle of this knowing?

MY REFLECTIONS:

Day 17

Discernment

"May the Lord bless his land...with the best gifts of the earth and its fullness and the favor of him who dwelt in the burning bush."

Deuteronomy 33:13-16

A friend once told me that he had never seen a burning bush, but he had learned to pay attention to many smoldering ones. By strengthening our sense of intuitive knowing, we may not be able to feel we are directly spoken to by God, but we are much more likely to experience a smoldering bush. Though we long to hear a message aloud from God, the lack of audible (either interiorly or exteriorly) messages does not foreclose the possibility of dialogue with what is greater than ourselves.

The Christian term Holy Spirit is often referred to as the Spirit of Truth. When our intuitive knowing gives us the sense of the truth about something, we are having a dialogue with something greater than ourselves. We may do a mental analysis and decide—yes, this is the course of action we should take. Then we sit with it, perhaps pray about it, and if we get back a sense of intuitive knowing that this is our truth, we have in fact been in a dialogue with something greater than ourselves. Or, we may have an idea of what we should do and we talk it over with a trustworthy friend. After our conversation with our friend, we are in a different perspective about the choices we face. We may see more possibilities and better options. Somehow something outside ourselves has given us a more truth filled perspective.

Occasionally such expanded knowing will point toward a smoldering bush. We will become aware that there is some opportunity, or idea, in our lives that is pulling us. It may not be God speaking to us directly, but we have a choice: we can neglect the smoldering or we can stay attentive to it. We can blow on the coals. We can see what opportunity may be offered to us that we have hardly been aware of.

<u>Practice</u>: Reflect on how you can engage in dialogue with a greater wisdom than yourself.

MY REFLECTIONS:

Day 18

Communion

"When he arrived and saw what the grace of God had done, he was glad and encouraged them all to remain true to the Lord with all their hearts."

Acts 11:23

Once we learn to be on the lookout for smoldering bushes, then we have the opportunity to develop different ways to communicate with what has not yet fully sprung to life in our lives. If our psychic house is cleared we can spend time in prayer and meditation—prayer, not of mental habit, but of our body, emotions and heart. This prayer brings all of us to a silent dialogue with God.

Often it is necessary to make one creative step forward with an open mind to receive back from the world a creative answer. Our actions become a form of dialogue with God.

Here is the formula. We take an action toward where our intuitive knowing pulls us. After the action we are aware of what is experienced. Is there a sense of rightness, of bringing more of our life to bear in the world? Or do we experience anger or upset?

Our actions, and our experience of those actions, is a form of dialogue that includes what is greater than ourselves. We see this when we experience an action, our reaction to that action and then have a knowing that is greater than the two. We experience that something of Beauty is created.

We now see how the old religious argument of faith versus works is misplaced. Our actions, what we do, are simply a part of a dialogue with what we believe. The deeper we get into that dialogue the more opportunity there is for Beauty, for Grace. Grace doesn't depend solely upon either. Rather discernment of Grace depends upon the dialogue. The dialogue is the opportunity for something new to enter our thoughts, feelings and lives. When it does we have an experience we call Grace.

Practice: Reflect on whether you are in monologue or dialogue? Can I listen to God through paying attention to my actions?

MY REFLECTIONS:

Day 19

Communion

"But the gift of God is eternal life in Christ Jesus our Lord."

Romans 6:23

Often as we progress along our spiritual paths, our beliefs become less and less important. Our faith becomes more grounded, not in a set of beliefs about God, but in the dialogue with God that our meditation, prayer and actions bring.

Beliefs have their attraction. They offer a sense of solidity in our minds that provides security. And we all need a certain amount of belief security to be able to start on our spiritual journeys. But as the dialogue between our faith and actions opens up new possibilities in our lives, then the meaning of our beliefs often becomes more fluid. It is as if our beliefs were the first stage rocket booster that was necessary to get us launched onto our spiritual journeys, but as we gain altitude and trajectory we are less dependent upon these beliefs to sustain our journey. The gravity of beliefs lessens. What becomes more important is our intuitive knowing that comes from our beingness. We are on the right path and in a dialogue of prayer and action. Almost inevitably once we are launched on our spiritual journey, if we grasp our beliefs too firmly, we restrict either our faith or our actions.

Practices: Reflect on whether your beliefs restrict the dialogue between your faith and your actions.

MY REFLECTIONS:

Day 20

Separation from God

"But the edges of our lives—fully experienced, suffered, and enjoyed—lead us back to the center and the essence."

Richard Rohr

Many middle class people have one of two responses to the church as an institution. They find that it is a good social institution, a nice place for their kids to go to day care and a nice place to meet people like themselves. Or, they react against and leave the church because they see it as filled with hypocrisy because it is a nice safe, social institution that is at odds with Christ's fundamental message of reaching out to and being at one with those suffering on the margins of life: the poor, those with social stigmatizing diseases like leprosy (today might be AIDS), the prostitutes (today maybe those with different sexual orientations), those of different racial backgrounds like the Samaritan, etc.

In the first case, the need to belong to feel socially safe in the world has gotten me to church, but once there, the church does not encourage me to follow Christ. In the second case, the need to feel socially safe by feeling superior through a judgment about who I am and who the marginalized are has prevented me from following Christ, in or out of church.

These are both ego traps—the ego's need to feel safe, the ego's quick judgment of superiority in order to feel okay. Both are false self defenses that keep us stuck, out of touch with our own authenticity and connection with God.

Our contemplative practices offer us a way out of this ego defeating box. Our centering prayer, welcoming prayer and daily examen offer us the chance to be aware of, to experience and to turn over to God the part of us that is marginalized, the edges in our lives where we are wounded, where we act like prostitutes and tax collectors.

Practice: Reflect today on how the institution of the church helps or hinders your faith journey.

MY REFLECTIONS:

Day 21

Separation from God

"Come to me, all you who are weary and burdened, and I will give you rest."

Matthew 11:28

Yes, Jesus' message was and is explicitly for the marginalized in society. But it was and is also for the marginalized part in each of us. That is—there are parts of us that are just as poor and outcast as any desperately poor person in a third world country. Until we recognize the dualistic dilemma of the church as a vehicle for Jesus' message and the dualistic way we see ourselves (focused on our good idealized image of ourselves and repressing our own anger and selfishness) we remain separate from the true meaning of Christ's message.

The way to wholeness—holiness—is through allowing God to integrate the marginalized parts of ourselves back to being centered in the ground of being, where we are not living from or out of our false selves (protective ego), but living from Christ within us and us in Christ. It is what Richard Rohr means when he often says much of the spiritual journey in the second half of life is about shadow work. Shadow work is important not because we can make ourselves better (ego self-improvement project) or so we can become more righteous (there is a big shadow) but so we can abandon ourselves to God's love. We can't abandon ourselves to God from a place of doing it all right, or thinking we are even good Christians. We can only abandon ourselves to God from our broken, fragile most human edge.

Practice: Today reflect on where in my life is my edge most torn? Can I go there and from there fall deeply into the embrace of God's Love?

MY REFLECTIONS:

Day 22

Separation from God

"Some people feel guilty about their anxieties and regard them as a defect of faith. I don't agree at all. They are afflictions, not sins."

C.S. Lewis

C.S. Lewis makes a profound distinction, which has great consequences for our contemplative journeys. Let's see if we can unpack his wisdom for our lives.

What are these afflictive anxieties that Lewis is talking about? The easiest understanding of them is found in what the Desert Father Ponticus Evagrius called the nine blocks to our connection with God. These afflictions, or blocks, that Evagrius wrote about (and seven of which were designated by the Pope in the 1200's as the Seven Deadly Sins) are what in modern terms we know as the nine points of the False Self on the Enneagram. In other words, we all bring our particular flavor of an affliction into our lives. The affliction is energy tied up in the ego, or False Self, which is trying on its own terms (which of course is the only terms the ego knows) to create the experience of the True Self—our authentic self connected to God. The corollary of the last clause is that only in connection with God is our True Self revealed and celebrated, as we are in Christ and Christ is in us.

What does this have to do with contemplation? Our Enneagram type provides us with a roadmap to understand the nature of our afflictive energy. During Centering Prayer this energy arises in our thoughts and feelings. As we let go of thoughts and feelings we experience the release of this afflictive energy. Similarly, Welcoming Prayer welcomes and transforms this energy by not resisting it. The afflictive ego energy of the False Self is just that—energy. Our contemplative practices are designed to free it from the energy harness of the ego and en-train this energy to move us toward God.

Practice: Today reflect on your awareness of the purpose of your contemplative practices? Are they dissolving separation from God?

MY REFLECTIONS:

Day 23

Separation from God

"A monk is a man who considers himself one with all men because he seems constantly to see himself in every man. "

Ponticus Evagrius

One of the great things about understanding the nine blocks to God, or afflictions as C. S. Lewis calls them, is that we are given a map showing us how human unhappiness in ourselves and others comes from this same nine-aspected source. With this map we see we are less separate from others. We experience greater compassion for others. And together these experiences of less separation and compassion lead us to being less separate from ourselves and from God. We are from the very beginning inexorably connected to our Creator; it is the ego unconsciously trying to re-create that experience of connection on its own terms that creates greater and greater levels of experienced separation.

Here are these nine afflictions that block us from connection with God.

Type One—Resentment

Type Two—Pride

Type Three—Deceit

Type Four—Envy

Type Five—Avarice

Type Six—Fear

Type Seven—Gluttony

Type Eight—Lust

Type Nine—Sloth

Practice: Reflect today on which afflictive energy is most active in your life.

MY REFLECTIONS:

Day 24

Separation from God

"As you uncover God's loving truth, you uncover your own, and as you uncover your own truth, you fall deeper into God's mercy and love."

Richard Rohr

The nature of fallen humankind is we all have this self-willed ego-self that has this ego driven energy. The nature of the energy for each of us is defined by type. We use our contemplative practices to convert (conversion) this energy to be in service of God's will for us. To do this we must first build awareness to see when our ego is calling the shots. To follow Lewis' distinction the affliction is not the sin, but sin arises from behavior resulting from the ego being in charge of the afflictive energy.

Thus for a type one, when the afflictive energy allows the type one to make a judgmental, a critical remark to feel okay—the remark is the sin. For a type two, to ingratiate oneself among important people to feel okay--the ingratiation is the sin. For a type three, to praise God for personal glory—the action of self-aggrandizing is the sin. For the type four, to fantasize about the future in order to avoid being present in the present moment—the fantasizing is the sin. For the type five, to refuse to share with someone who needs—the non-sharing is the sin. For the type six, the refusal to forgive out of fear that if forgiveness is given betrayal might happen again—the refusal to forgive is the sin. For type seven, the letting down of a friend because your afflictive energy caused you to overbook—the letting down the friend is the sin. For the type eight, the barging ahead to get the job done regardless of the effect on others—the oblivious barging ahead is the sin. For the type nine, the withdrawal afflictive energy causing you to fail to engage with what or who you love—the failure to engage is the sin.

Our contemplative practices help us re-direct the energy which comes with our affliction away from behavior that falls short and into conscious action to serve something greater than our small self.

<u>Practice</u>: Reflect on where the afflictive energy of your type most often leads you to fall short.

MY REFLECTIONS:

Day 25

Separation from God

"When my being opens up inside of the safety and spaciousness of God, it always invites me into deeper and daring honesty, deeper self-surrender, deeper shadow work with my own illusions and my own pretensions."

Richard Rohr

One of the great fruits of contemplative prayer is that when we give our emotions and thoughts time to settle down, where we miss the mark—that is where we have acted out the afflictive energy in order to feel okay—becomes patently clear.

Thus, one of the fruits of contemplative practice is we see where we need to make amends for wrongs we have caused. Much of the time the severity of a wrong has a time component to it. In other words, the longer the wrong is allowed to fester the more harm it causes.

For the Enneagram type one, the longer the pattern of critical remarks goes on the more harm it causes. For the two, the longer the two tries to manipulate others to feel okay the greater the co-dependency that is created. For the three, the longer the self glorification goes on the harder it is for the three to see the self-deceit. For the four, the more the four longs for the idealized past or future, the greater the disconnect with others. For the five, the longer one refuses to share, the greater the suffering caused. For the six, the longer one goes without forgiving, the greater the suffering of the one who needs forgiveness. For the seven, the longer one keeps creating more options, the more another suffers from being an object of inconstancy. For the eight, the longer one pushes relentlessly ahead the more harm that is done to others. For the nine, the more one avoids addressing disagreement the more separation occurs.

Our contemplative practices give us a chance to break the energy of our afflictive patterns earlier. When this happens the harm is stopped and we can use this energy to make amends, to correct the harm we have caused. When we do this, we not only restore a right relation with another we have harmed, we restore a right energetic relation with God.

Practice: Reflect on where I need to make amends for wrongs caused by my afflictive energy.

MY REFLECTIONS:

Day 26

Separation from God

"Like all afflictions, they are, if we can so take them, our share in the Passion of Christ."
C. S. Lewis

Because the Enneagram has its origins as a spiritual tool, those afflictive energies that block us from experiencing our connection with God are called passions. Biblically, we understand the Passion of Christ to be his suffering on the cross. There are several different ways that the church tries to explain Jesus' death and resurrection theologically. Some of these explanations may be of help to some of us, to others perhaps hindrances.

But separate and apart from the theological niceties, what Lewis is telling us is that we are in this with Christ—our suffering from our afflictive energy is a part of what Christ has also suffered. It is in the solidarity of suffering that redemption occurs. We are not alone. Our creator is right there with us all the way. It is in waking up to the reality of this redemption that we discover that not only are we not alone but we live and breathe in God's love.

It is through our contemplative practices that we see that the letting go of our afflictive energies is a necessary death, for only then is that energy converted into service to do God's will. When we see doing for others as "stuff" we should do, we are probably just trying to do God's will from an ego point of view. No harm done often, but we have not de-constructed the false self energy—that is we have not allowed ourselves to experience the solidarity of suffering with Christ. When the solidarity of this suffering has occurred, the energy is converted (conversion) and doing God's work flows naturally. Like cats whose behavior is all cat-like behavior; when our energy flows from God not our ego, we are God's creatures in God's will doing god-like behavior. We aren't trying to do good, good just flows from that authentic connection with God.

Our contemplative practices allow us to develop this sensitivity to the experience of our energy. We begin to see whether the actions flow from our ego self or our connection to God.

Practice: Reflect on where your energy to do good comes from?

MY REFLECTIONS:

Day 27

Separation from God

"People who go deeper with God invariably have a very honest evaluation of themselves. They are never proud people. They can't be, because the closer you get to the Light, the more you see your own darkness."

Richard Rohr

In the Enneagram scheme of looking at our patterns of energy, our conversion causes our passion to be converted to our virtue. The word virtue comes from the Latin *virs* which means life force or virility. In other words conversion frees the energy trapped in the ego's scheme of managing our safety and survival. When the *virs* is freed, our life force is freed so that our energy flows freely and continuously from our Creator. We no longer need the illusion of safety the ego creates because we are dependent on God. Yes, of course we get tired at times because we are human creatures, but we don't get tired because we spend all our time managing our emotional and mental energy.

The conversion of our energy from our passion to our virtue by Enneagram type is:

Type one—resentment converts to serenity

Type two—pride converts to humility

Type three—deceit converts to authenticity

Type four—envy converts to equanimity

Type five— avarice converts to non-attachment

Type six—fear converts to faith

Type seven—gluttony converts to sobriety

Type eight—lust converts to innocence

Type nine—sloth converts to engagement

Our contemplative practices give us the chance to learn to identify the nature of our energy, to see when it is stuck in our passion and when our life is flowing from our virtue.

<u>Practice</u>: Reflect on where and how your energy get converted from your passion to your virtue.

MY REFLECTIONS:

Day 28

Separation from God

"But the fruit of the Spirit is love, joy, peace, forbearance, kindness, goodness, faith-fulness, gentleness and self-control."

Galatians 5: 22-23

If we allow our life energy to unconsciously run our lives we never get the chance to see if we are living from our passion or from our virtue. Our contemplative practices allow us to become aware, to see where our energy is coming from, to learn what is the energetic feel of what our energy is creating. In Galatians Five we are given instructions as to what is the fruit of the Spirit. In other words, what is our experience when our actions flow from the Spirit, which necessarily means the energy has been converted from our passion to our virtue. Galatians Five gives us an after-the-fact litmus test. From a contemplative stance, where we are not identified with our ego, we can hold up our actions and observe where the energy of the action came from by looking at what is the quality of the field that was created.

As you can see the Galatians litmus test refers to nine aspects of the fruit of the Spirit. These correspond with the nine aspects of the Enneagram. So here is a chart showing the conversion of false self energy to the virtue and the resulting fruit of that *virs* or life force.

Type one—resentment converts to serenity, the fruit of which is long-suffering

Type two—pride converts to humility, the fruit of which is meekness

Type three—deceit converts to authenticity, the fruit of which is goodness

Type four—envy converts to equanimity, the fruit of which is love

Type five—avarice converts to non-attachment, the fruit of which is joy

Type six—fear converts to faith, the fruit of which is more faith

Type seven—gluttony converts to sobriety, the fruit of which is temperance

Type eight—lust converts to innocence, the fruit of which is gentleness

Type nine—sloth converts to engagement, the fruit of which is peace

Practice: Reflect on where in your life you experience the fruit of the Spirit that comes from the conversion of your passion energy to your virtue.

MY REFLECTIONS:

Day 29

The Way of the Marginalized

"Now when Jesus saw the crowds, he went up on a mountainside and sat down. His disciples came to him, and he began to teach them. He said: "Blessed are the poor in spirit, for theirs is the kingdom of heaven. Blessed are those who mourn, for they will be comforted. Blessed are the meek, for they will inherit the earth. Blessed are those who hunger and thirst for righteousness, for they will be filled."

Matthew 5:1-6

Liberation theology recognizes in the Gospels what has been called a preferential option for the poor. Jesus' Way involves speaking most directly to the prostitutes, the tax collectors, the Gentiles, those that are on the margins.

Not surprisingly we see that the Christian message has thrived in those places where people are poor and oppressed, from the Roman repressed state in which Jesus lived to modern day church movements in Africa and Asia.

So how does a middle class American find the Way in this message to the marginalized. We find it because we all have a part of ourselves that we have marginalized. It is through our recognition of this marginalized place that Grace can enter and transform our middle class lives. So the Way involves building an awareness of our own broken and marginalized aspects. The Way is a way of whole-ness. It is reclaiming the marginalized parts of ourselves that gives us wholeness, i.e. holiness.

The Enneagram is a wonderful tool for us to use to see where our marginalized parts are. The wonderful thing, about building this greater awareness of our marginalized self, is because slap up against our wounded part is often the most important gift we have.

Practice: Reflect on what parts of me are the marginalized.

MY REFLECTIONS:

Day 30

The Great Give-a-way

"Come to me, all you who are weary and burdened, and I will give you rest. Take my yoke upon you and learn from me, for I am gentle and humble in heart, and you will find rest for your souls. For my yoke is easy and my burden is light."

Matthew 11:28-30

The church has often made the message of Jesus seem overburdened with guilt and must-dos. How is the Way an easy Way?

It has to do with giving up the energy tied up in the false self. Giving up the energy tied up in keeping our personality looking perfect, doing the right thing, performing for approval, etc. When this energy is converted (conversion) then indeed the Way is easy.

We are not doing this good deed for someone because we "should" or the "Bible tells me so." We do it because the energy of our small self has been converted so we stand in our ground of Being with God. When our energy is not tied up in our personality, then there is plenty of energy, love, good deeds to give away. In fact, what we see from Jesus is that it just flows naturally. So naturally that people are healed just by touching the hem of his garment.

The Way is easy when our ego is not in charge, and God is running the show. How simple and how at times dauntingly difficult. The key to converting this energy from self energy, to God's continuous flow is meeting God at our marginal edge. This is the place conversion occurs.

<u>Practice</u>: Reflect on whether you are trying to live a good life or whether you are surrendering so God is doing good things through you.

MY REFLECTIONS:

www.ingramcontent.com/pod-product-compliance
Lightning Source LLC
Chambersburg PA
CBHW080529030426
42337CB00023B/4673